DATE DUE		

Your Government:
How It Works

The Environmental Protection Agency

Daniel E. Harmon

Chelsea House Publishers
Philadelphia

CHELSEA HOUSE PUBLISHERS
Editor in Chief Sally Cheney
Director of Production Kim Shinners
Creative Manager Takeshi Takahashi
Manufacturing Manager Diann Grasse

Staff for THE ENVIRONMENTAL PROTECTION AGENCY
Assistant Editor Susan Naab
Production Assistant Jaimie Winkler
Picture Researcher Jaimie Winkler
Series Designers Keith Trego, Takeshi Takahashi
Cover Designer Takeshi Takahashi
Layout 21st Century Publishing and Communications, Inc.

The Chelsea House World Wide Web address is
http://www.chelseahouse.com

First Printing
1 3 5 7 9 8 6 4 2

Library of Congress Cataloging-in-Publication Data

Harmon, Daniel E.
  The Environmental Protection Agency / by Daniel E. Harmon.
    p. cm. — (Your government—how it works)
Includes bibliographical references (p.   ).
  ISBN 0-7910-6792-0
  1. United States. Environmental Protection Agency—Juvenile literature. 2. Environmental protection—United States—Juvenile literature. 3. Environmental policy—United States—Juvenile literature. I. Title. II. Series.
TD171 .H37 2003
                                            2002000143

Contents

YOUR GOVERNMENT HOW IT WORKS

Introduction

Government: Crises of Confidence

Arthur M. Schlesinger, jr.

FROM THE START, Americans have regarded their government with a mixture of reliance and mistrust. The men who founded the republic understood the importance of government. "If men were angels," observed the 51st Federalist Paper, "no government would be necessary." But men are not angels. Because human beings are subject to wicked as well as to noble impulses, government was deemed essential to assure freedom and order.

The American revolutionaries, however, also knew that government could become a source of injury and oppression. The men who gathered in Philadelphia in 1787 to write the Constitution therefore had two purposes in mind: They wanted to establish a strong central authority and to limit that central authority's capacity to abuse its power.

To prevent the abuse of power, the Founding Fathers wrote two basic principles into the Constitution. The principle of federalism divided power between the state governments and the central authority. The principle of the separation of powers subdivided the central authority itself into three branches—the executive, the legislative, and the judiciary—so that "each may be a check on the other."

YOUR GOVERNMENT: HOW IT WORKS examines some of the major parts of that central authority, the federal government. It explains how various officials, agencies, and departments operate and explores the political

5

organizations that have grown up to serve the needs of government.

The federal government as presented in the Constitution was more an idealistic construct than a practical administrative structure. It was barely functional when it came into being.

This was especially true of the executive branch. The Constitution did not describe the executive branch in any detail. After vesting executive power in the president, it assumed the existence of "executive departments" without specifying what these departments should be. Congress began defining their functions in 1789 by creating the Departments of State, Treasury, and War.

President Washington, assisted by Secretary of the Treasury Alexander Hamilton, equipped the infant republic with a working administrative structure. Congress also continued that process by creating more executive departments as they were needed.

Throughout the 19th century, the number of federal government workers increased at a consistently faster rate than did the population. Increasing concerns about the politicization of public service led to efforts—bitterly opposed by politicians—to reform it in the latter part of the century.

The 20th century saw considerable expansion of the federal establishment. More importantly, it saw growing impatience with bureaucracy in society as a whole.

The Great Depression during the 1930s confronted the nation with its greatest crisis since the Civil War. Under Franklin Roosevelt, the New Deal reshaped the federal government, assigning it a variety of new responsibilities and greatly expanding its regulatory functions. By 1940, the number of federal workers passed the 1 million mark.

Critics complained of big government and bureaucracy. Business owners resented federal regulation. Conservatives worried about the impact of paternalistic government on self-reliance, on community responsibility, and on economic and personal freedom.

When the United States entered World War II in 1941, government agencies focused their energies on supporting the war effort. By the end of World War II, federal civilian employment had risen to 3.8 million. With peace, the federal establishment declined to around 2 million in 1950. Then growth resumed, reaching 2.8 million by the 1980s.

A large part of this growth was the result of the national government assuming new functions such as: affirmative action in civil rights, environmental protection, and safety and health in the workplace.

Some critics became convinced that the national government was a steadily growing behemoth swallowing up the liberties of the people. The 1980s brought new intensity to the debate about government growth. Foes of Washington bureaucrats preferred local government, feeling it more responsive to popular needs.

But local government is characteristically the government of the locally powerful. Historically, the locally powerless have often won their human and constitutional rights by appealing to the national government. The national government has defended racial justice against local bigotry, upheld the Bill of Rights against local vigilantism, and protected natural resources from local greed. It has civilized industry and secured the rights of labor organizations. Had the states' rights creed prevailed, perhaps slavery would still exist in the United States.

Americans are still of two minds. When pollsters ask large, spacious questions—Do you think government has become too involved in your lives? Do you think government should stop regulating business?—a sizable majority opposes big government. But when asked specific questions about the practical work of government—Do you favor Social Security? Unemployment compensation? Medicare? Health and safety standards in factories? Environmental protection?—a sizable majority approves of intervention.

We do not like bureaucracy, but we cannot live without it. We need its genius for organizing the intricate details of our daily lives. Without bureaucracy, modern society would collapse. It would be impossible to run any of the large public and private organizations we depend on without bureaucracy's division of labor and hierarchy of authority. The challenge is to keep these necessary structures of our civilization flexible, efficient, and capable of innovation.

More than 200 years after the drafting of the Constitution, Americans still rely on government but also mistrust it. These attitudes continue to serve us well. What we mistrust, we are more likely to monitor. And government needs our constant attention if it is to avoid inefficiency, incompetence, and arbitrariness. Without our informed participation, it cannot serve us individually or help us as a people to attain the lofty goals of the Founding Fathers.

CHAPTER 1

Poisoned Water, Poisoned Air, Poisoned Earth

NATIVE AMERICANS IN days of old called it "Cuyahoga," or "Crooked River." In 1969, *Time* gave it a much more scornful name: the river that "oozes." The U-shaped waterway over many years had become thick with oil and floating trash as it flowed through **industrial** northern Ohio, passing Cleveland and emptying into Lake Erie. It was not exactly appealing to swimmers or fishermen, but most people accepted the river's condition with a resigned chuckle or a sigh of disgust.

Then the unimaginable happened: The water caught fire. Beginning in 1936, a series of smoldering fires changed the Cuyahoga from a river that stank to a river that actually burned. When a glowing, flowing blaze lit the Cuyahoga in 1969, national attention focused on the once-beautiful river—and on a growing problem in America: **pollution**.

Why Are Rivers Polluted?

The Environmental Protection Agency (EPA), the U.S. government department founded to address the problem of pollution, estimated that in

1989 at least 10 percent of America's waterways were polluted, some more than others. It found that more than 17,000 rivers, streams, and coastal regions were **contaminated**.

What are the contaminants? There are two types: those caused by nature and those introduced by humans. Bacteria and algae are natural contaminants found in rivers. When you visit a wilderness area in Africa, South America, or even closer to home, you usually are warned, "Don't drink the water!" That's not necessarily because the local people have polluted it. Rather, it may be that the water contains living, microscopic *organisms*. Typically, people who live there have grown accustomed to the water over a long period of time, so they are not harmed by certain local bacteria. They are **immune**. However, if your body is unfamiliar with these organisms, they can make you very sick.

Even in your own local **environment**, some natural contaminants can be dangerous. An example in the news during recent years is the E. coli bacteria. It lives in the intestines of certain animals and humans. That means it can be passed into the environment either in human sewage or in natural animal waste. People have become ill not only by drinking contaminated water, but also by swimming and playing in lakes and rivers that contains E. coli and certain other germs.

More worrisome today than natural contaminants, though, is pollution caused by humans. In rivers, pollution commonly comes from factory, city, and community waste and drainage systems. Among other elements, lead and other poisonous metals have affected our water supplies. Chemicals, including insecticides and cleaning liquids, find their way into rivers and lakes, sometimes with serious results.

The Cuyahoga is just one of thousands of polluted waterways. Many of the others are much larger and longer than the Cuyahoga. One river to come under heavy criticism by **environmentalists** has been the great Mississippi, which extends almost the full length of the American Midwest, north to south. Since numerous other sizeable rivers and

small streams enter the Mississippi after they pass through more than a dozen states, the Mississippi's contaminants come from countless sources.

One Part of a Much Larger Problem

Although rivers are only one part of our environment, they are often the scenes of environmental controversies. For generations rivers have absorbed more than their fair share of pollution. Many factories were built at riverside to take advantage of the benefits that waterways had to offer. In the early years of industrialization, one of those benefits was obvious: A moving body of water seemed to be nature's perfect garbage disposal. Dump the company's waste products into the swift-moving current, and soon they were swept from sight and forgotten.

For a while, this worked to the satisfaction of most people. Indeed, it was hardly noticed. Industrial waste of the 19th century was only a fraction what it would become during the 20th century. Americans rarely spoke the word "pollution."

In 1952 the large amounts of flammable chemicals in the waters of the Cuyahoga River in Ohio spontaneously ignited. The fire destroyed boats, three buildings, and the ship repair yards.

Furthermore, the public a hundred years ago didn't suspect or understand all the problems industrial waste—chemical waste in particular—could cause for a river, its wildlife, and its surroundings. If fish were discovered belly-up 10 or 20 miles downstream from a factory, or if people occasionally got sick from eating the fish they caught in the river, few guessed the cause might be unnatural chemicals in the water. Fewer still imagined those chemicals came from a factory that operated perhaps miles away.

Even after biologists and others began to investigate river pollution, it took a while for them to prove that the source of that pollution was humans and human industries, not nature. Almost invariably, when suspicion of pollution was leveled at an industrial facility, the factory owners would deny blame and point to other, usually natural, causes.

Finally, by the time we admitted that some of our manufacturing operations truly were contaminating the environment, we had come to depend on those factories. They were producing goods the public needed and wanted, and they were providing jobs people desperately needed. Their success affected the nation's economy. Many people in government and industry, as well as in the community, argued that a certain amount of pollution would have to be allowed, for the overall good of the people.

But how much? That's one of the issues in which the EPA gets involved. Its job is to monitor the nation's environment and ensure that nature is not overtaxed by the demands of a growing, industrialized society.

Grappling with a Monster

River pollution is one example of the EPA's tough challenge. Also polluted are many of our lakes and seacoasts. Accidents involving offshore oil platforms and oil (or chemical-carrying transport ships) cause widespread, long-lasting problems. An infamous example was the 1989 wreck of the *Exxon Valdez*, an oil tanker that grounded on a reef off the Alaska coast. It spilled 258,000

Accidents involving oil and chemical tankers and offshore oil platforms are devastating to wildlife living both in and around the affected body of water. On April 15, 1989, the Exxon Valdez *oil tanker spilled approximately ten million gallons of crude oil off the Alaska coast. This accident caused extensive long-term damage to the environment.*

barrels (more than ten million gallons) of crude oil into the ocean, polluting more than a thousand miles of coastline. For months afterward, viewers watched heartrending news tapes and photos of stricken aquatic and bird life as workers labored to clean up miles of grimy shoreline. The estimated toll included 100,000 dead birds and at least a thousand sea otters. As appalling as these death tolls sound, however, worse environmental disasters have occurred. The *Exxon Valdez* wreck was not even among the 10 worst oil spills on record.

Oil and chemical spills and industrial or municipal dumps aren't the only threats to our waters. Ordinary citizens pose hazards to wildlife (and to humans). Sea turtles have been found choked to death on plastic bags. Swimmers and waders are injured—sometimes very seriously—by broken glass and jagged, rusty cans half-buried underwater. Waterside and wilderness dumping and littering by families and individuals are sadly common.

Concern also has focused on our soil. Pollution of the earth can affect not only the food we produce but also our natural groundwater supply. It can also endanger wildlife. Insecticides, for instance, help farmers grow healthy crops—but some of these chemicals have been proved poisonous to the earth. Even more chilling is the threat of radioactive pollution. **Radioactivity** is a by-product of nuclear energy, on which Americans have come to rely for part of their power needs. Radioactive elements and waste are extremely dangerous, lasting hundreds, thousands, or even millions of years before they decay into safe elements. They're also difficult to dispose of.

And then there's the very air we breathe. Millions of vehicles across America each day send poisonous exhaust into the air. Combined with industrial vapors, they damage the quality of our atmosphere. Some of these air-borne **toxins** settle onto the crops we grow or are soaked into the ground by rain. Some hover in the air we breathe. And some rise miles above the earth's surface to the edge of space. Scientists warn that this form of pollution may be changing the very nature of the earth's protective canopy, causing long-term problems such as "global warming," a process by which the atmosphere warms to the point of changing the earth's climate.

Since its creation in 1970, the EPA has been the U.S. government's answer to the growing environmental crisis. How well has it policed our natural surroundings?

Some critics complain it has not done enough or has acted too slowly to resolve and prevent crises. Some officials in industry, city government, energy production, agriculture, and automotive design, on the other hand, argue that certain EPA policies are needlessly strict.

Water, soil, air—the three basic ingredients of our planet. All have come under severe pressure from a growing human population. In this book, we will examine how the Environmental Protection Agency is trying to protect our planet's most precious natural resources.

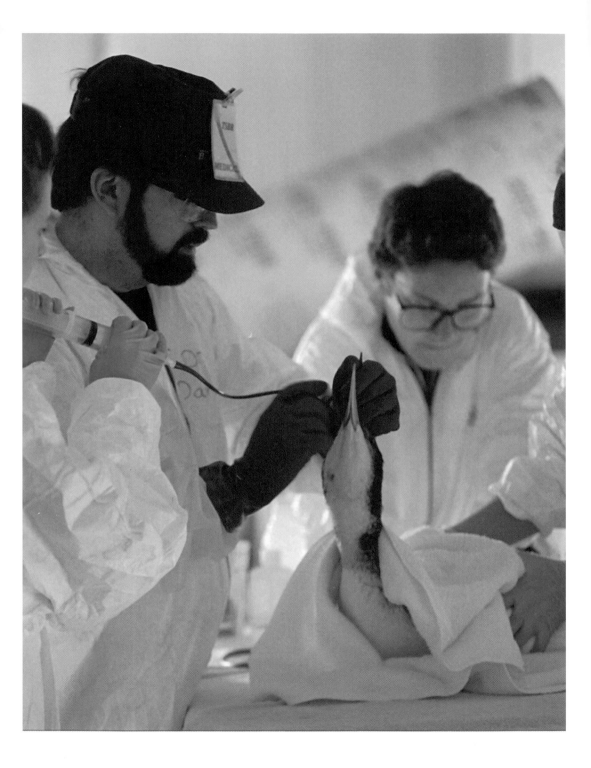

A loon (bird) was covered in oil from a spill in South Kingston, Rhode Island on January 22, 1996. It is critical to the ecological balance of an area that every effort be made to save animals from such man-made destruction.

CHAPTER 2

Tinkering with Ecology—a Brief History

PROTECTING OUR ENVIRONMENT is more complicated today than ever before. To understand what is involved, we need to understand the meaning of a scientific term: **ecology**. This refers to the way humans and other animals, as well as plants, are related to and interconnected with one another and with the nonliving world around them.

Did you know that there are approximately *5 million different kinds of animals and plants* on our planet? Some are very large, including elephants and hippopotami. Some are microorganisms, so tiny we can see them only with powerful microscopes. Others (like us) are in between.

It may seem hard to believe that, on a planet with 5 million species, removal or reduction of just one type of plant or creature can dramatically affect the other types of life. But any alteration in a species population can produce a dramatic or subtle change to an **ecosystem**. In some instances, humans never feel the impact of these changes. Sometimes the effects are enormous and eventually involve thousands of species—but only in a local area, such as an island or an isolated region of a continent. In other cases, though, upsetting nature's ecological balance spells disaster for both wildlife and people in nearby communities and even throughout whole countries.

Human population growth, which exploded during the 20th century, has changed the ecological picture radically. Today, approximately 6 billion people inhabit the earth—twice as many as there were only 40 years ago. Some of the things humans do are harmful to animal and plant life; the larger the population, the more harm humans cause. For example, when we clear land to build houses or plant new fields, we take away the **habitat** of the creatures that lived there before. When we pollute the earth, water, and air, we poison plant and animal life, perhaps to the point of extinction. Human pollution harms humans, as well.

Environmental and Health Practices in Early America

Almost immediately after the first Europeans began building settlements in America, they saw the obvious need for what we today might call "basic environmental control." Sewage regulations were the most pressing concern. Colonial governments in the 1600s began issuing edicts forbidding the opening of privies (early toilets, usually separate from houses) too close to settlers' forts or to public wells or other water supplies.

Soon, they found it necessary to control the garbage disposal habits of citizens and tradesmen, particularly butchers and tanners. As early as 1684, the Massachusetts General Assembly authorized fines against slaughterhouses and butcher shops that were not kept reasonably clean. Colonial legislatures began providing for official scavengers, men who would remove and bury dead animals—which in the early settlements sometimes were left to rot on vacant lots and even in the street.

Dirty Streets and Drainage

The first government efforts to regulate public health matters were opposed by settlers who had come to America

Ultimately we could become the victims of our own thoughtless pollution and abuse of the earth's environment and natural resources. When we harm the air, water supply, soil, animal life, and plant life that surround us, how long will it be until we, too, suffer directly?

in search of freedom. Most early Americans believed they should have the right to do whatever they wished, even if it jeopardized the public good. When the city of Pittsburgh, Pennsylvania, in the early 1800s passed an ordinance making it illegal to throw garbage in the streets, citizens angrily protested. Well into the 19th century, many Americans refused to keep their hogs, horses, and other livestock in pens. They let them roam in public.

Most U.S. cities by 1830, however, had found it necessary to keep their streets reasonably clean. They appointed street "commissioners" or ordered local boards of health to oversee street cleaning, either by citizens or by hired workers.

Sewage was a much more serious problem than street litter. Poor families living in crowded slums did not have adequate bathrooms. Simple pots and bowls had to be used for toilets, their contents dumped into neighborhood gutters. Gutter drainage found its way into streams, rivers, and sometimes wells—the public water supply. Early American water mains were made of wood, which leaked and rotted. The first cast-iron pipes, introduced in Philadelphia, Pennsylvania, were not used until 1818.

Dirty Air

When the first signs of air pollution rose over American industrial centers, most residents paid little heed. The ones who did were not certain whether smog might be harmful or helpful. In 1826, a report on living conditions in Pittsburgh described a dark, "sulfurous canopy" over the city that sometimes made it hard to see. A leading Pittsburgh doctor suggested the chemicals in the air were "antiseptic," helping prevent the spread of disease and providing "relief" to people with asthma.

By the mid-1800s, however, many Americans—especially those living in major industrial cities—were unhappy with air pollution. Interestingly, their concerns were of a different nature from those we have today. Modern scientists warn of many complex problems that stem from a polluted atmosphere. Back then, doctors and health pioneers did not have the knowledge or the evidence that would come only with generations of worsening air quality. Their great fear was that contagious diseases were caused by polluted air and poor ventilation in crowded cities and buildings. One doctor in 1874 described to the American Public Health Association what he called the "crowd-poisoned atmosphere" of cities. If it continued to worsen, he warned, it would spread typhus and other fevers.

We know now that poisonous air is not generally the culprit in spreading epidemics. Nonetheless, it is certainly dangerous. In London, England—long noted for its frequent foggy conditions—almost 4,000 people died in 1952 as a result of an extended period of thick "smog" (smoke combined with fog). Some perished in auto accidents caused by almost zero visibility. Others died of asthma attacks and other breathing-related problems. In America, a similar

Since the early 1900s man has been burning gasoline to power automobile engines. This is a view of the San Francisco Bay Bridge in California. The Texas Transportation Institute annual statistics show that people living in the San Francisco-Oakland, California, region spent forty-two hours per year in traffic in 1999. This was an increase from thirty-eight hours per year in 1997.

though less dramatic situation had occurred four years earlier in Donora, Pennsylvania.

Events of that nature are rare, but smog is common, especially in large cities. People from small towns and rural areas are often shocked when they approach a heavily populated metropolitan area by airplane and observe the brownish haze into which they are descending.

The Environmental Protection Agency has identified hundreds of poisons in our air today. How has the atmosphere become polluted? Largely, it becomes polluted from the use of energy. Automobiles and trucks burn gasoline. These vehicles, which came into increasing use in the 1900s, release exhaust fumes into the air. Often you can see smoke puffing from the exhaust pipes of automobiles and trucks. Even if you don't see it, poisonous exhaust is coming from all vehicles on the highway.

In addition to exhaust, unhealthy gasoline fumes rise into the atmosphere before the gas is ever used. When gas and oil are transferred from one storage container to another, a small portion is lost. The simple process of filling your car tank with gas releases gas fumes into the air. The more people inhabiting planet earth, the more traffic on our roads. The more traffic, the greater this problem becomes.

Meanwhile, factories and utilities burn energy on a much larger scale, and emit large volumes of poisonous waste from their smokestacks.

Nature has a way of fighting air pollution. Trees and other plants can filter much of the carbon and other exhaust poisons from the air through a process called **photosynthesis**. But nature is unable to keep up with the increasing human population and its increasing consumption of energy.

Dirty Water

Street filth has contributed to America's drinking water pollution for centuries. Polluted air also increases the pollution of water. Much of the poisonous matter in the air eventually settles. Rainfall brings it down to coat plant life and flow into streams and lakes.

Pollutants in some water supplies include chemicals from pesticides and fertilizers used on farms. Rain washes these chemicals into water sources beneath the soil. Eventually, they enter rivers and lakes, and from there become part of public drinking water systems. EPA tests have found, for example, that an alarming number of wells in the United States contain high levels of nitrates, which are likely the result of fertilizer compounds leaking into the groundwater.

Meanwhile, fertilizer residue creates a different kind of problem in some streams and lakes: It helps algae grow. Algae are a natural part of wetlands and serve a useful purpose. Out of balance, however, they can consume a body of water and stifle other life forms.

Farmers and industries aren't the only culprits. In the past, and even in modern times, water pollution can be traced to ordinary citizens and communities. For years, many towns and cities in America placed their sewage-processing plants at waterside. Why? So they could channel the town's sewage—either treated or raw—into a peacefully flowing current that would take it downstream and out of sight. Unhappily for the homes and towns downstream, the sewage becomes their problem.

An outhouse in Clarkson, Kentucky, emits raw sewage directly into a stream that feeds Nolin Lake. Many sewage-processing plants were located by the waterside of major cities so waste could be directly discharged into the water and flow downstream with the current. This kind of short-term thinking proved highly dangerous for our environment.

Poisonous Waste

Beyond the immediate danger of chemical use in our modern society lies the problem of toxic (poisonous) waste. Toxic waste includes unusable chemicals and metals from factories, automotive oils and acids, and radioactive waste material from nuclear facilities—not to mention unsafe items and substances that we throw away with our household garbage.

Most waste goes into landfills, liquid reservoirs, and pits. Some is flushed into sewage systems. Some is poured into rivers. After we dispose of these poisons, we forget about them—but the planet can handle only so much dumping without suffering serious injury. It can take many lifetimes for certain poisons to "go away," fully absorbed by nature.

In our next chapter, we'll look further at our garbage disposal dilemma and at other threats to our planet.

A photograph taken in October 1975 showing Theater Alley off of Park Row, located near New York's City Hall. Clearly the garbage disposal rules in this section of the city were not being strictly followed. A crowded urban area, such as the one in this photograph, needs to control the disposal of waste or risk causing a serious health hazard to the city's population.

CHAPTER 3

Our Damaged Environment

VIRTUALLY EVERYONE AGREES that our mounting environmental problems result primarily from the world's burgeoning human population. The more people living on the planet, the more human waste—sewage, common garbage, chemical emissions from energy production—is cast into the wild that we expect nature to handle. At the same time, humans have needs that must be met. Supplying the population with food is a simple example. We can increase crop yields by using fertilizer to make vegetables and fruits grow and pesticides to protect the crops from weed and insect damage. However, the more chemicals we use in agriculture, the more polluted our surroundings become. The challenge for governments is to find ways to care for growing populations—allow industries to operate and farmers to farm—without destroying our environment.

Just what are the long-term issues of environmental damage? Let's examine several basic ones.

Severing Food Chains

Scientists long have known that food sources for humans and animals are linked in succession. They call it the "food chain." Simply put, plants anchor the chain, providing edible food for insects (as well as for some species of large animals). Insects are eaten by mice, lizards, snakes, and other reptiles and fur-coated creatures. More powerful animals feed on these creatures, and larger animals, in turn, feed on them.

Take away the plants—even just a few especially important food plants—and the entire food chain is threatened. Take away any link in the chain, and the links above it are in trouble.

Humans do many things that disrupt food chains— some of which seem necessary to us. In many parts of the United States at certain times of year, for example, we perform large-scale spraying to control pesky mosquito populations. This seems desirable to people, but it is not so desirable to the birds and other creatures that feed on mosquitoes, because it eliminates much of their food supply.

Pest control—and pollution—can affect higher food chain links in another way. Animals that eat sprayed or polluted plants, or eat insects poisoned by our insecticides and chemical waste, take those poisons into their bodies. Larger animals then eat the smaller ones, and so on. Humans ultimately eat some of the animals whose flesh contains poisons that humans themselves applied to the environment. In the aftermath of the 1986 Chernobyl nuclear disaster in the Ukraine (discussed later in this book), people across Europe worried about eating meat and drinking the milk of livestock that grazed on grass contaminated by radioactive fallout.

When chemicals enter the soil, either deliberately or accidentally, they can stop the growth of some or all of the area's plant life. And as we've seen, plants are the basis of the food chain.

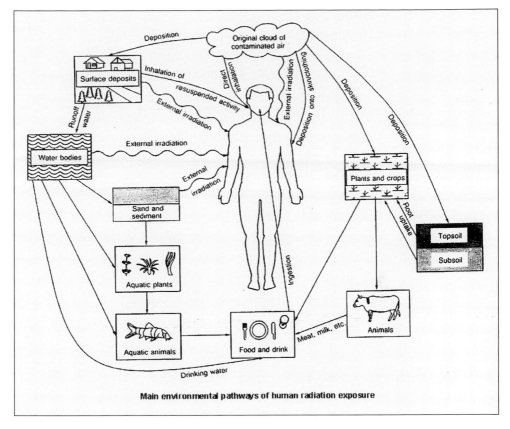

Main environmental pathways of human radiation exposure

Hazards to Human Health

Pollution looks bad and smells bad, but is it really harmful to our health? Definitely. We still don't know the full effects on humans of exposure to low but constant levels of hazardous elements, but evidence shows that higher levels of exposure can cause or worsen certain types of health problems. In the London smog debacle of 1952, many of the almost 4,000 deaths were caused by lung ailments, including asthma. Asbestos, a material once used commonly for insulation, has been shown to contribute to cancer and to cause a type of progressive lung disease. (The Environmental Protection Agency estimated that during the early 1980s, as many as 10,000 American deaths a year were caused by asbestos-related lung cancer.) PCBs, chemicals once popularly used in electric and gas systems, were banned in the late 1970s after research linked them to birth defects and cancer.

Pollution can harm us through various physical channels. This diagram of a man illustrates how we can be affected: through the food we eat, the water we drink and bathe in, the soil our fruits and vegetables grow in, and the radiation emitted by nuclear waste into the atmosphere.

Particulate poisons—ashes and chemical particles that contribute to air pollution—can be so strong that they corrode steel and concrete structures. The potential damage to human skin and lung tissue is painfully easy to imagine.

On-the-job safety became an explosive political and legal issue by the late 20th century. Apart from the presence of hazardous materials and conditions in some working environments, buildings of modern design are nearly airtight. If not ventilated and filtered properly, such buildings can pose serious health hazards to the people inside them. These buildings came to be known as "sick buildings." Ironically, some of the offices housing the new Environmental Protection Agency by the mid-1980s were found to have polluted interiors.

This situation brought home an alarming point: In the long run, humans cannot expect to find shelter from the pollution they create.

Garbage Disposal—the Big Picture

Some regions of the country today are concerned about the availability of **landfill** space in the future. Landfills are massive open sites where household garbage is dumped and periodically covered over with layers of dirt. Eventually, the entire site is filled, and a new disposal site must be found.

Since garbage accumulates evermore rapidly in our heavily populated and growing cities, dumping space eventually becomes a serious problem. Only certain types of land are suitable for safe dumping. For example, areas prone to erosion and flooding are not suitable as landfill sites because garbage and harmful chemicals might eventually be released into the surrounding area. Also, certain types of soil are not very effective for reclaiming trash as it decomposes.

Can landfills ever be reused? Only in a limited sense. When a site finally is covered over and closed to dumping, authorities plant trees and ground cover. Some sites then can be used safely for recreational purposes. Construction usually is forbidden, however, because as

the trash rots deep in the earth, it makes for an uneven, unstable building foundation.

An alternative to landfills is **incineration**—burning trash rather than burying it. Waste material is not completely destroyed, however, even by intense flames. It creates smoke that can pollute the atmosphere (and ultimately, when it settles, the earth and water). Also, ash remains that is exceptionally high in hazardous content such as lead and cadmium. Ash is usually dumped in landfills. Although the volume and weight of ash is far less than that of unburned garbage, ash contains more concentrated poisons. Disposed ash, some environmentalists point out, is easily absorbed into groundwater and, if not secured quickly, scattered into the air, posing an even greater danger to the environment than ash buried in ordinary landfills.

Another severe problem is the disposal of chemical waste. Until the mid-1900s, companies were not particularly careful about dumping hazardous waste. The public, not

Landfills are vast spaces in the ground that are filled with garbage and covered with dirt. But with time, landfills are filled to capacity and new ones must be found. This is a picture of a landfill in Amelia County, Virginia. On February 9, 1999 the Virginia State Senate approved a bill which, among other things, limited the growth of such landfills.

Decades of dumping chemicals in the Love Canal in the City of Niagara Falls, New York, resulted in a toxic slurry that forced families living in and around the area to evacuate their homes. The governor of New York declared Love Canal a disaster area. Here a child who lived near Love Canal protests on August 5, 1978.

suspecting major health and environmental problems from improper chemical disposal, seemed to care little about where companies disposed of their industrial waste.

The practice came under widespread criticism in 1978-1979 when hundreds of families had to be evacuated from their Niagara Falls, New York, homes near the Love Canal. The uncompleted barge canal site had been a chemical dump throughout the 1940s. Thirty years later, it was found to be "leaking" a variety of dangerous chemicals into the air and water. High rates of birth defects and certain forms of cancer were recorded among area residents. The governor of New York declared Love Canal a disaster area. Other chemical dump sites in the region also were found to be emitting poisons.

When the government began imposing restrictions on dumping in the early 1970s, some cities sent their waste out to sea to dump it. Garbage—including dangerous medical waste—washed ashore in 1988 along public beaches in New Jersey and New York, forcing officials to close beaches.

Time to Take Notice

For generations, most Americans denied or ignored the ever-increasing problem that environmental pollution was becoming. This attitude is hardly surprising, since practically every individual was contributing in some way to the mounting pollution crisis. No one wanted to admit responsibility. But the effects of pollution couldn't be ignored forever. It was taking its toll. Sooner or later, society would have to confront the problems brought on by a burgeoning human population on the earth's ecology.

CHAPTER 4

The Government Steps In

AS AMERICA ENTERED the 1900s, local health departments and agencies were responsible for dealing with most environmental problems. Usually led by doctors in the community, these early health agencies were concerned mainly with fighting and preventing the spread of dreaded diseases, with the hope of avoiding **epidemics**. Eventually, they began to look at broader problems that might be caused when humans became too careless with their surroundings.

Although the efforts of these health officials were praiseworthy, they were often misguided, because of the lack of sound information about environmental hazards. For instance, during the late 1800s, some health departments ordered utility companies not to dig ditches for water, gas, or telegraph lines during the summer. Their theory was that disease causing bacteria lived in the subsoil and would thrive and spread if they were released into the hot, humid air by digging.

American society was beginning to make real progress in building sanitary water and sewer systems by the turn of the 20th century. Many growing cities, though, could not meet the needs of their growing populations. Meanwhile, other environmental problems had arisen.

Time for Serious Action

In 1899, Congress passed a significant (although barely effective) law intended to prevent the buildup of pollution in America's waterways. The Rivers and Harbors Act banned liquid dumping in navigable waters (waters used for transportation and commerce). Sewage was not included among the restricted liquids, and the law was not well enforced. It was almost half a century later that the Water Pollution Control Act of 1948 revisited the issue, authorizing the U.S. Department of the Interior to intervene against polluters and providing federal funds for cities and towns to construct sewage treatment facilities. In 1955, Congress passed the Air Pollution Control Act, getting the Public Health Service involved in pollution research and control.

Public concern over environmental dangers was growing rapidly. In 1962, a book called *Silent Spring* by biologist Rachel Carson became a bestseller. It warned of the dangers of, DDT, widespread pesticide use. In the coming years, more and more readers took Carson's warning to heart. They expressed concerns about what pollution of all forms, not just pesticides, was doing to our planet. Pollsters found that in 1965, fewer than 20 percent of Americans believed the government should begin a major initiative to address pollution problems. By 1970, however, more than 50 percent of Americans were rating pollution a top issue.

Biologist Rachel Carson warned of the dangers of pesticides to our environment in her book Silent Spring *(1962). Her book led to the study of pesticides and their effects on the environment. Here she speaks to Congress about regulating the sales of chemical pesticides and reducing the amount of aerial spraying of pesticides.*

A major step toward pollution control was passage of the Air Quality Act of 1967. It provided federal guidelines for monitoring and guarding the quality of the air we breathe. It set no national standards, however. Local governments could decide for themselves what should be done to improve

air quality—and for the most part, they decided to do little.

The federal government was beginning to press for environmental clean-up in other areas. During the late 1960s, it began ordering cities to stop flagrant pollution of waterways. For example, it ordered sewage facilities in Iowa to treat their waste before discharging it into the Mississippi and Missouri river system. It ordered city officials in Toledo, Ohio, to stop municipal pollution of Lake Erie.

The Earth Gets Its Day and a Watchdog Is Born

Senator Gaylord Nelson of Wisconsin was the motivating force behind what was to become an annual event: Earth Day. Some 20 million Americans—an unexpectedly large turnout—took part in demonstrations, educational programs, and debates during the first Earth Day on April 22, 1970. In its aftermath, local and national environmental organizations were created. Since 1970, Earth Day each year has drawn attention to new and existing environmental problems and possible solutions.

Even before the first Earth Day, the federal government was putting an environmental plan into gear. President Richard M. Nixon in 1969 formed the Environmental Quality Council, a panel to advise him on the full range of pollution concerns. Congress, wanting more than a presidential advisory council to address the problem, drafted a broad, national environmental policy in a landmark piece of legislation. Nixon signed Congress' National Environmental Policy Act several months before Earth Day. If new construction projects were to qualify for federal funding, the act required their planners to study the impact these projects might have on the environment. Furthermore, it created a special agency to enforce related laws: the Environmental Protection Agency (EPA). President Nixon appointed

The organizers of the first Earth Day on April 22, 1970 sought to focus public attention on problems with the environment and address and solve these problems. In this photograph, taken on the second Earth Day in 1971, we see bicyclists riding down Fifth Avenue in New York City to commemorate the day.

William D. Ruckelshaus as the agency's first administrator.

The EPA did not have to "start from scratch." Already in existence were various small government programs and bureaus within five different federal agencies, all devoted to certain aspects of environmental concerns. Transferred to the EPA, they included a number of research groups monitoring pesticides, water quality, and **radiation**. Taken together, the Environmental Protection Agency began its mission with a $1.3-billion budget and more than 5,000 employees.

But what, exactly, was to be its mission? In President Nixon's mind, the EPA should set and regulate environmental standards, research environmental issues, and assist other government bodies involved in environmental protection matters. Today, the EPA's mission, stated simply, is "to protect human health and to safeguard the natural environment." Specifically, the agency "provides leadership in the nation's environmental science, research, education and assessment efforts; makes sound regulatory and program decisions; and carries out effective programs and policies to improve the global environment." It coordinates its efforts with those of state and local governments. Ideally, industries cooperate with the government to abide by environmental standards set by the EPA. If they do not, the agency must use its authority to ensure a safe environment.

The duties of the Environmental Protection Agency are many and complex. For example, it sets standards for treating, storing, transporting, and disposing of hazardous waste. The EPA approves or rejects state agency proposals for cleaning up air pollution in their regions. Under the guidelines of the Clean Water Act of 1972, the EPA must protect not just humans but aquatic life forms, as well, from water pollution. The agency determines the levels of toxic waste that industries and cities can discharge into waterways without disrupting nature. It also monitors the condition of **groundwater**, the underground sources of well water and natural springs, and of drinking water outlets. It protects wetlands (marshy coastal areas and swampy fringes of lakes and river regions) as well as waterways.

New Laws Give the EPA Its Teeth

A powerful federal agency was ready to go to work on behalf of the environment. First, though, it needed enforceable laws to back its efforts. Until 1970, America's laws in that regard were somewhat vague and left many loopholes for polluters to continue their activities. Happily for the fledgling agency and for the country, the mood was right for a string of meaningful new legislation.

The Clean Air Act of 1970 set standards designed to control 189 different air pollutants from industries and automobiles. For example, it required industrial facilities to install filters on smokestacks and automakers to install exhaust-reducing devices on cars and trucks. Oil companies were ordered to market unleaded gasoline.

In 1972, Congress passed the Clean Water Act. This legislation required factories and city utility plants to reduce the pollution they were discharging into waterways and lakes and to make already-polluted public waters safe for swimming and fishing. The Marine Protection, Research, and Sanctuaries Act, passed the same year, authorized the EPA to police the dumping of sewage and poisonous chemicals into the sea. The Water Pollution and Control Act was amended, giving the EPA control over all U.S. waters.

Also in 1972, the EPA was ordered to police a different form of pollution: noise. Congress' Noise Control Act ordered the EPA to set standards for noise levels produced by construction equipment, auto engines, and other loud machines. (Airline noise was placed under the monitoring of the Federal Aviation Administration.) In addition, the 1972 Environmental Pesticide Control Act mandated that makers of **insecticides** and **herbicides** register their products with the EPA.

The Safe Drinking Water Act, further empowering the EPA to guard America's water supply, followed these laws in 1974. The Resource Conservation and Recovery Act, regulating hazardous waste disposal, was passed in 1976. Under it, the agency can monitor waste at every stage, from its appearance to its treatment and eventual disposal. The Toxic Substances

Congress set up the "Superfund" in 1980 to finance the clean up of abandoned waste sites. This Superfund was financed with tax money obtained from chemical producers. This is a photograph of Blue Mountain, along the Lehigh Gorge in Palmerton, Pennsylvania. The EPA has been trying to clean up eighty years' worth of environmental damage caused by smelting by the Zinc Corporation of America.

Control Act was passed the same year, authorizing the EPA to police industrial chemical use. The Energy Policy and Conservation Act in 1978 gave the EPA the power to set pollution standards for new automobiles.

In 1980, Congress adopted the Comprehensive Environmental Response, Compensation, and Liability Act, which became known as the "Superfund." This act taxed the producers of certain chemicals, using the taxes to set up a trust fund for the EPA to use in cleaning up abandoned dumps that contained poisonous waste. In 1986, in answer to a growing alarm over the disease-causing potential of asbestos, Congress passed the Asbestos Hazard Emergency Responses Act. This legislation ordered schools to comply with EPA standards pertaining to asbestos levels; in some cases, it meant asbestos materials had to be removed from school buildings.

The original Clean Air Act was amended in 1990 to impose stricter regulations on air pollutants. Also in 1990, in the aftermath of the *Exxon Valdez* oil spill, Congress passed the Oil Pollution Act, threatening heavy fines on oil companies responsible for oil pollution disasters.

The Environmental Protection Agency is charged with administering such laws. It carries out its responsibilities both directly and through state environmental agencies that operate locally, following EPA guidelines. Some states have passed their own laws that set even stricter rules on land, water, and air pollution than the federal government.

The Need for Individuals to Participate

Up until the early 1970s, most Americans did not seem to take fuel and pollution issues seriously. (In any case, they made little effort to cut down on their personal use of fossil fuels.) All this would change by 1973, however, when the oil-producing countries of the middle east reduced their shipments of oil to the United States, which was using imported oil to meet a third of its oil and gasoline demands. The result was a gasoline shortage that reached all the way to the retail pumps. Many gas stations literally had

no gas to sell, and many of those that did increased their prices and limited the amount of gas that a customer could buy at one time. Lines of cars and trucks jammed the streets of U.S. towns and cities as drivers waited to obtain a few gallons of a once-ordinary item that suddenly had become precious.

Fuel "conservation"—a term that had seemed vague and boring to the average citizen—became very important. Car-pooling was encouraged, and many people bought small economy cars to cut down on their gas purchases. The government reduced the speed limit on superhighways to a rate at which cars ran more efficiently, and ordered car manufacturers to begin producing cars that burned less gas and emitted less harmful exhaust. To lower their consumption of heating and cooling energy, people began keeping their homes cooler in cold weather and warmer in hot weather.

A negative result of the 1973 oil crisis was that many Americans, worried about the availability of fuel, seemed to lose interest in environmental protection issues. Perhaps, they reasoned, higher levels of pollution would have to be tolerated for energy providers to meet public heating and fuel demands.

Once the 1973-1974 crisis passed, many Americans returned to their old, energy-wasteful habits, to the dismay of environmentalists. Today, few seem to remember the long gas lines of 1973. Author Laurence Pringle has surmised, "When the entire United States cuts its use of petroleum, its citizens will save money. They will breathe cleaner air. And North America's rivers, bays, and beaches will suffer less from those double disasters, oil spills."

In the 1970s fuel conservation strategies included driving small, fuel-efficient cars, reducing the speed limit to energy-efficient levels, and lowering the thermostat in the winter. This picture from September 1973 shows people in northern California lining up for gasoline during a time of government-imposed gasoline rationing.

This photograph shows smog over the city of Los Angeles, California. Smog is the result of excessive pollution in the air and consists of sulfur dioxide, carbon monoxide, and suspended particles of pollutants.

CHAPTER **5**

Waging a Smelly —and Deadly—War

AMERICA'S LARGE METROPOLITAN areas are at risk from several major categories of air poisoning, according to the Environmental Protection Agency. These include sulfur dioxide (a result of burning sulfurous coal), carbon monoxide (most of which comes from auto exhaust), oxidants (also attributed to exhaust), and "total suspended particulates" (ranging from wind-blown dust and flower pollen to soot from chimneys).

But poisoned air, while the most widely noticeable form of pollution, is just one part of the EPA's battle. Let's look at several other major concerns.

Fertilizers and Pesticides: Necessary but Dangerous

As you probably know from your studies in science, plants draw nourishment—water and many important chemical elements—from the soil in which they grow. When our ancestors cleared and planted fields for the first time, the land was "virgin" soil, whose mineral content had not yet been tapped. With each planting season, however, more of the

Crop dusting planes are used to spray synthetic fertilizers, pesticides, and herbicides on crops.

original minerals that the crops used for growth became depleted. Over time, farmers were faced with the problem of "poor soil" that no longer could support healthy crops.

How could they restore necessary chemicals to their lands? The answer was **fertilizer**. Fertilizer is a form of chemical (often a blend of two or more chemicals) that can be spread over the field and absorbed into the dirt, either by plowing or rain saturation. Through the 1800s, our ancestors relied on natural fertilizers, including bones, wood ashes, and animal waste—manure or bird droppings—all of which are rich in certain chemicals. Massive farming operations of the 20th and 21st centuries, however, call for mass-produced, **synthetic** fertilizers. Modern fertilizers contain different ingredients. Most common soil additives are nitrogen, potassium, and phosphorus.

In an earlier chapter we learned about the harm that fertilizer can cause to our waterways and reservoirs when it washes into them. Synthetic fertilizer has another disadvantage. Unlike natural fertilizers, synthetics do not add **humus** to the soil. Humus is decayed but solid animal or plant matter (the old-fashioned, natural fertilizers). While lending chemical nourishment, it also improves the texture of topsoil, helping it store moisture. Without it, rain and irrigation water quickly sink down into the water table below.

Fertilizers aren't the only farming chemicals that find their way into our drinking water supplies. Great quantities of pesticides are sprayed on growing crops—herbicides to prevent the growth of unwanted plants amid the vegetables and fruits, and insecticides to prevent bugs and other animal life that eat or otherwise damage the crops. Some of these chemicals, too, wash into and through the soil, draining into streams, rivers, and well water sources. Meanwhile, birds and other animals eat some of the raw, treated crops growing in the fields, taking the potentially deadly chemicals into their systems. The pesticide called DDT was blamed for the radical reduction of the bald eagle and peregrine falcon populations during the late 20th century. Eagles and falcons don't raid crops, but they feed on rodents, which feed on insects. Insects were poisoned by the DDT; rodents were poisoned by the insects; birds of prey were poisoned by the rodents.

Pesticide traces are sometimes found in the fresh produce consumed by humans. Among other dangers, certain cancers have been linked to pesticide poisoning.

Interestingly, many kinds of insects and bacteria over time have become immune to pesticides that once were effective in controlling them. Environmentalists openly wonder whether certain pesticides now are more harmful to animals and humans than they are to the tiny "pests" they're supposed to kill.

Oil and Water

The EPA reports that thousands of oil spills occur each year in American waters. Only a few cause major damage. But for a society that depends heavily on **fossil fuel**, oil shipments account for much of the commerce being transported to American ports by ship, and offshore oil wells are kept busy. Potential tanker and oil rig accidents make work dangerous for the crews. They can spell catastrophe for our wildlife and ecosystems.

In effect, the cost of a massive oil spill is threefold: (1) the loss of precious oil, (2) the cost of clean up, and (3) the toll it takes on nature. The greatest monetary cost is in clean-up operations. A "barrel" of oil holds 42 gallons of crude. Depending on circumstances, it can cost the government and private companies more than a thousand dollars per barrel to clean up an oil spill—far more than the oil is worth.

In terms of the environment, the losses never can be counted fully. In some situations, oil contamination actually kills fish. In others, fish do not die directly from the oil, but scientists find that the pollution kills tiny water creatures on which fish feed. It also can change fish life cycles and reduce their ability to protect themselves from natural predators. The same is true of waterfowl and their food chains. It even can affect humans, if they eat seafood that has been contaminated.

We read earlier of the *Exxon Valdez*, the tanker that spilled a fifth of its cargo of oil off the Alaska coast in 1989. Human error was blamed for the disaster. Other spills have had many other causes. The sea itself is a dangerous place, as the crew of the supertanker *Metula* learned in 1974. Their vessel went aground off the southern tip of South America in the Strait of Magellan, a passage known by mariners the world over for its treacherous currents and tidal rushes. More than 50,000 tons of crude oil from Arabia spilled from the *Metula's* tanks into the sea, killing ocean life and polluting 50 miles of Chilean coast.

In North American waters, tanker ship disasters date to World War II, when German submarines prowled offshore. The *Esso Gettysburg* was torpedoed off Savannah, Georgia, in 1943. Apart from the loss of 57 crewmen, it poured almost 120,000 barrels of crude oil into the sea. An engine room explosion took down the *George MacDonald* off the Atlantic coast in 1960. Its loss: 130,000 barrels of fuel oil. In 1969, the towing cable broke between an oil barge and its tugboat at Cape Cod. When the barge ran aground, 25,000 gallons of diesel fuel flowed from a hole in its bottom. The pollution was so devastating that shell fishing had to be stopped in the area for five years.

Accidents happen at both onshore and offshore oil drilling sites. In 1979, a malfunction at a well in the Gulf of Mexico poured approximately half a million tons of oil (about 13 times the amount spilled by the *Exxon Valdez*) into the sea. The site was 50 miles offshore, so damage along the gulf shoreline was only moderate. The consequences for aquatic life in the Gulf, however, were enormous. It took workers almost 10 months to cap the well.

Alarming news headlines bring such disasters to our attention. Not all oil pollution, however, results from disasters. Much of it occurs during the normal course of work with tankers and pipelines. Oil is sometimes spilled while being piped. Ship crews frequently flush their oil storage tanks after a voyage. While laws forbid the discharge of oily water in and around American ports, certain tankers have been suspected of flushing oil containers at sea. And some small boat owners contribute to the problem by dumping used motor oil into the water illegally.

The sea also is polluted by rivers that empty into it. They

The governor of New Jersey, Christine Todd Whitman (R), now head of the EPA, walks along Sunset Beach in Cape May, New Jersey after an oil spill in the Delaware Bay. Massive oil spills waste precious oil, cost millions of dollars to clean up, and cause serious damage to the environment.

bring down a Pandora's box of municipal and industrial waste from discharge points far inland. For many years, Americans assumed the rivers and oceans were so vast they could easily absorb waste products with little or no effect. Now we understand the error of this thinking.

Chemical Hazards New and Old

One problem challenging the 21st-century EPA is that hundreds of new chemical compounds are introduced by manufacturers each year. Some have never been fully tested, and the agency lacks the resources and staff to keep up with developments. In the words of one commentator: "Often the burden of proving harm from toxins falls squarely on the shoulders of citizens."

In the meantime, old hazards must be monitored and controlled. The earth-shattering calamity of September 11, 2001, brought home that concern to citizens in and around New York City and Washington, D.C. After terrorist attacks destroyed the twin towers of the World Trade Center in New York and damaged the Pentagon in Washington, one of the environmental concerns was the presence of asbestos fibers and toxic particles spread from the fiery ruins. These dangers threatened people who live and work near the disaster sites and, especially, the thousands of rescue and clean-up workers at the scenes.

Environmental Protection Agency staffers quickly went to work monitoring air content. They found little cause for concern at the less damaged Pentagon but detected low asbestos levels in the World Trade Center ruins. Working with officials from the federal Occupational Safety and Health Administration, they advised relief workers in safety measures. For example, firemen kept the massive debris piles wet during the cleanup period to limit the quantity of dust rising into the atmosphere. Meanwhile, 10 EPA vacuum trucks drew away dust from the disaster site. Agency officials closely monitored the debris as it was cleared away and moved to nearby Staten Island.

The ruins of the World Trade Center in New York City were a potential source of hazardous pollution to rescue workers and people who lived or worked in its vicinity. In this photograph workers vacuum sand at the Washington Market Park on Sunday, September 30, 2001. The sand was tested and shown to contain asbestos. Inhabitants of the area surrounding the World Trade Center disaster site wondered if they should wear breathing masks as the cleanup ensued.

"Should we wear breathing masks?" New Yorkers wondered. EPA test reports assured them that while workers in the restricted cleanup area needed to use respirators for safety, pollution levels did not suggest a need for people in nearby districts to wear such devices.

The Environmental Protection Agency and New York City environmental officials also tested drinking water in New York and the Potomac River area of Washington and Virginia to determine whether the disasters had caused contamination. The agency issued an all-clear report.

In response to a larger concern over possible terrorist attacks on the nation's water supply, the EPA declared that "the water supplies in the United States are among the safest in the world and the threat of mass contamination is small." The government agency makes sure city and private water suppliers have effective plans in place for emergencies. "In the unlikely event of a terrorist act, the plans typically call for shutting down the water supply system, notifying the public through the mass media, providing an alternate source of drinking water or providing consumers with information on how to treat the water to make it safe—boiling, for example." The agency points out that public water system authorities are legally required to monitor water quality and notify the public if the water is found to be unsafe.

Concern over America's drinking water supply is not new. One dangerous pollutant, arsenic, enters water systems naturally. Contained in rocks and soil, arsenic traces can be released into the environment as a result of normal erosion. In recent years, the EPA has required water suppliers to limit the arsenic content in drinking water to 50 "parts per billion." After more recent studies, the agency in 2001 tightened the regulation, allowing no more than 10 parts per billion of arsenic after 2005.

Nuclear Power: Blessing or Curse?

A series of scientific experiments and discoveries over a period of 50 years climaxed in the harnessing of atomic, or **nuclear**, energy during World War II. Its first use, prompted by the U.S. government's desire to win and end the six-year-long world conflict (1939–1945), was the making of bombs. The first two atomic bombs, which the United States dropped on Japanese cities in 1945, indeed forced the Japanese to surrender.

After the war, the United States and other countries set about developing nuclear power further. They built arsenals of incredibly powerful nuclear weapons. At the same time, they developed nuclear facilities to generate electrical power for the world's growing population. Nuclear energy, they found, could provide great amounts of power very cheaply and, in some ways, more cleanly than older power sources, including coal and oil. In 1957, the nation's first nuclear power plant began demonstrating the potential, creating ample electric power for Pittsburgh, Pennsylvania, with very little pollution. Over the next 25 years, the government licensed 86 other nuclear plants. In certain areas of the country, including New England, they began to generate more than half the citizens' electric power needs. (Overall, they were generating about 13 percent of the nation's electricity.)

However, nuclear power generation can cause problems. Uranium and plutonium, the source elements of nuclear energy, emit radiation, which can damage and destroy human tissue.

Nuclear power plants are heavily shielded to prevent radiation from escaping into the environment. Total protection is impossible, though. Traces of radioactive particles pass from nuclear facilities into the surrounding water and air. Just how much radioactivity do Americans encounter? That question constantly worries critics of nuclear energy. The nuclear industry says radioactivity accidentally released from power plants is so slight that it poses no threat. Opponents counter that radioactivity sometimes reaches dangerous levels, and that workers inside nuclear facilities are at great risk. They also point out how difficult it is to dispose of radioactive waste material. It takes many years for radiation to "go away." Radioactive waste must be very carefully stored and guarded.

Furthermore, as nuclear power plants age, radioactivity

The harnessing of nuclear power was achieved in the early 1940s by U.S. scientists, who were racing to build the first atomic bomb. In 1945, the United States dropped nuclear bombs on two Japanese cities, Hiroshima and Nagasaki, forcing the Japanese to surrender in World War II. In this grim photograph, Japanese survivors in Hiroshima wait for first aid attention.

builds up. Experts say each nuclear facility should be closed after about 40 years. Taking apart a highly radioactive power plant is no simple matter. Scientists and engineers have debated the safest way to "retire" nuclear plants. Most agree the process will be costly and will require years to complete.

Meanwhile, modern society lives in danger of a major accident involving a nuclear reactor at a power-generating facility. The reactor is a terrific power source—which means anything that goes wrong with it can trigger terrific danger. Unmanageable volumes of radioactivity can be released, spreading contamination and death near and far. The worst-case accident at a nuclear power facility is a meltdown of its reactor core. Because of the severe heat it generates, the core constantly must be water-cooled. If a problem arises with the cooling system, the reactor core can become so hot it literally melts, spreading radiation into the earth and atmosphere.

The first major nuclear plant disaster occurred in England in 1957. In the United States, partial meltdowns occurred in 1961 near Detroit, Michigan, and—in a far more serious event—at Three Mile Island in Pennsylvania in 1979. The world's worst nuclear accident to date occurred in 1986 at Chernobyl in the Ukraine. More than 30 people died immediately in fires and explosions; they were only the first in a long-term series of related deaths that never can be counted fully. Cancer deaths and birth defects probably linked to radiation from Chernobyl still are occurring and are expected to number in the tens of thousands. Some 135,000 people were evacuated from nearby towns after the accident.

Still, some energy experts believe nuclear power is the country's best alternative for the 21st century, especially in regions where hydroelectric (water-generated) power development is not practical. Despite the potential for catastrophe, it offers many advantages and is clean, compared to burning coal and oil.

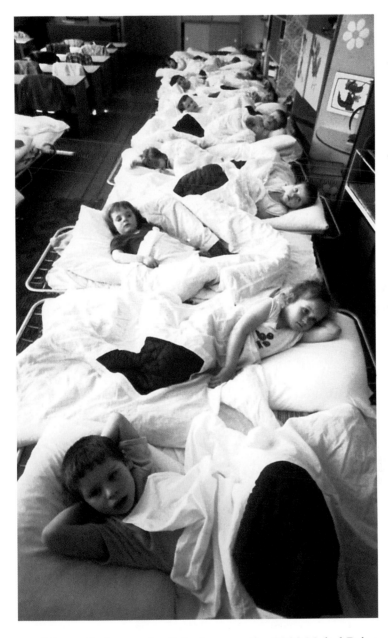

In 1986 at the Chernobyl nuclear plant in the Ukraine, the world's worst nuclear power accident in history occurred. The former Soviet Union did not release complete information about the accident to the world. Although we know of thirty deaths immediately following the first explosion, it is likely that tens of thousands more people may be suffering from the long-term effects— such as cancer and birth defects—of this accident. The children in this 1990 photograph are suffering from intestinal problems caused by radiation exposure, not far from Chernobyl.

Pierre Curie, a scientist who won the 1903 Nobel Prize in physics for his studies of radioactivity, expressed his belief that "humanity will obtain more good than evil from the new discoveries." Supporters and critics of nuclear energy have debated that issue for the last 50 years.

CHAPTER

6

Working for a
Cleaner Future

THE ENVIRONMENTAL PROTECTION Agency often finds itself
caught in the "politics" of environmentalism, both internationally and at
home. Some environmentalists have accused the EPA of making decisions
in favor of energy producers. Some energy producers and industries, on
the other hand, have accused the agency of being overbearing and making
it harder for them to develop products and serve their customers.

American environmentalists take little comfort in the fact that
compared to many other countries, the United States, through laws
and the efforts of such organizations as the EPA, is a leader in trying
to protect natural surroundings. The progress we've made, they
argue, has been too little and too slow.

Critics contend that the EPA often depends on industry-sponsored
testing to decide whether and to what extent chemical use should be
restricted. Biased testing procedures and, at times, deception have
been discovered in the past, as certain chemical companies have

sought to keep potentially hazardous substances in production. Independent testing is more likely to expose hazards, environmentalists argue. Some within the EPA openly agree, but point out that the agency lacks the funding to pay for more independent research.

It isn't simply a debate of progress versus environment, but also of region versus region. One of the issues is who bears the responsibility for pollution and its cleanup—the originator or the victim. This question arises when, for example, acid rain falls and brings environmental damage in one area . . . but the acid came from hundreds of miles away. For example, in 1984, authorities in Pennsylvania, New York, and Maine formally asked the EPA to require seven Ohio River Valley states to their west to reduce air pollution that was affecting precipitation patterns in the Northeast. The EPA denied the request on the ground that the agency lacked full authority to resolve the matter.

A See-Saw Battle

During the 1980s, the administration of President Ronald Reagan streamlined government departments. The EPA's staff and budget were cut by approximately one-fourth. In 1983, after just more than two years in office, EPA Administrator Anne Gorsuch Burford resigned under pressure, amid charges of mismanagement and contempt of Congress. The agency's reputation as an effective environmental watchdog suffered. However, Congress during the Reagan presidency substantially increased its Superfund waste clean-up support amount from $1.6 billion for the fund's first five years to $8.5 billion. And in 1986, the EPA vigorously attacked the problems caused by lead poisoning, reducing the allowable levels of lead in drinking water.

President George Bush, Sr., elected in 1988, proposed strong measures to improve air quality. His plan called for 50-percent reductions in sulfur pollutants from coal burning power plants and encouraged experimentation in the use of less harmful auto fuels.

The EPA has been criticized for biased, industry-funded testing. These critics believe that if the EPA paid for independent research, the results would most likely reveal more of the true hazards lurking in our environment. Here we see Dr. Bernhard Prinz, director of Air Pollution Effects and secretary of the State Institute for Pollution Control of Northern Rhine and Westphalia in Germany. Dr. Prinz planned to meet with fellow German colleagues and representatives from the U.S. Forest Service and EPA representatives at Westphalian forest damage research sites.

Despite all efforts, the scope of problems yet to be solved is enormous. For example, in 1994, the agency reported that approximately 40 percent of American waterways and lakes it surveyed were "too polluted for basic uses."

As it enters the 21st century, the agency faces a challenge far different from that of 30 years ago. In its 2000 Strategic Plan, the EPA pointed out that the "easy victories"—correcting blatant, highly visible incidents of pollution—have been won, and now a more difficult task awaits. "Increasingly, the EPA is finding that traditional approaches and regulation of large and obvious sources of pollution are not sufficient to achieve our goals nor the results the American people expect. We must also adopt new perspectives, try new approaches, and create new partnerships in our core environmental programs. . . . Today, it is no longer enough to focus only on controlling pollution. We face new problems, such as the loss of biological diversity and global climate change, which are much more difficult to assess and manage."

The EPA has 10 regional offices spaced throughout the nation. These offices help state, county, and city governments in controlling pollution. The agency's original staff of just more than 5,000 has grown to more than 18,000. They include biologists, chemists, oceanographers, pharmacologists, botanists, and toxicologists; safety, civil,

Christine Todd Whitman has been the administrator of the EPA since January 2001. Here she addresses the West Virginia Chamber of Commerce Business Summit in White Sulphur Springs, West Virginia. She boasts that the state of the natural environment has improved over the course of the last thirty years.

mechanical, nuclear, electrical, petroleum, and computer engineers; safety officers; civil and criminal investigators; planners; administrators; mathematicians and statisticians.

Christie Whitman, a former governor of New Jersey, became administrator of the EPA in January 2001. Whitman had built a regional reputation as an environmental leader during her seven years as New Jersey's governor. As EPA administrator, she advocates "smart growth" and believes the nation's economic and environmental concerns are closely linked.

Whitman says the Environmental Protection Agency has a simple goal: "to make our air cleaner, our water purer, and our land better protected." She adds, "Many people are surprised to learn that the condition of America's environment has actually improved significantly over the past 30 years—and is still getting better. Much work remains to be done, however, and the path to continued environmental improvements will require a new emphasis on partnerships. Some of the most creative solutions to our problems are generated at the local level by citizens, businesses, state and local governments, and other interested organizations, and we all need to work together to achieve the next generation of environmental progress."

America's Environment Then and Now

The first European colonists in America had little need to worry about ecological issues. There were relatively few humans—Native Americans and colonists combined—and much unoccupied land all around. Clearing space for fields and villages drove out the wildlife, it was true, but the animals did not have to move very far to find new habitats. The only environmental concern the settlers had was maintaining a reasonably sanitary, healthy community. As for the natural world around them, it easily could take care of itself.

With America's growing population and the coming of the Industrial Age with its many coal-burning factories, our society confronted the issue of pollution during the 1800s. A full century passed, however, before citizens began urging their government to do something about the problems. Only during the 1960s did we really begin to understand the damage human carelessness was doing to nature and to realize that these practices eventually would effect us as well as our wildlife.

As we enter the 21st century, Americans worry not just about environmental problems in our own cities and nation, but around the world. Scientists warn that air pollution from many countries is affecting the upper atmosphere. Worldwide threats created by this situation include damage to the protective ozone layer that encompasses the earth at the edge of space, which means more harmful ultraviolet rays from the sun reach the earth's surface. At the same time, the **greenhouse effect** increases the temperature within the earth's atmospheric canopy. This can bring about global warming, causing polar ice to melt and ocean levels to rise, and dramatically changing the climates of every region on earth.

The EPA voiced concern about gradual global warming in a 1983 report, predicting a rise in average temperatures

The protective layer of the atmosphere known as the "ozone layer" has been irreversibly damaged throughout the years. Some environmental scientists theorize that this damage may cause an increase in average temperatures on earth. This theory is known as the "greenhouse effect." In this photograph, protesters in Cleveland, Ohio, wear gas masks to show their anger about polluted air in their community. They are trying to rally local officials to increase measures to protect their air quality.

of several degrees during the 21st century. If that occurs, the agency stated, serious problems could present themselves by 2040, and by the year 2100 they could be "catastrophic." The agency urged increased study of the problem, as well as "innovative thinking and strategy-building."

At its Internet site today, the EPA devotes a special section to global warming information. It notes that climatic changes brought about by global warming can affect crop production and water supplies, while the sea level along most of the United States coast may rise two feet during the 21st century. "Today, action is occurring at every level to reduce, to avoid, and to better understand the risks associated with climatic change," the EPA states. "Many cities and states across the country have prepared greenhouse gas inventories; and many are actively pursuing programs and policies that will result in greenhouse gas emission reductions."

Public Involvement Makes a Difference

In an ideal world, individuals, groups, and businesses whose actions create problems would take on the task of correcting these problems, as well. In the real world, however, corrections typically are not made until people unite in protest and demand relief. The EPA, like most government offices, has been moved to action by public pressure in the past. At the same time, it depends on citizens to alert it to problems that otherwise might never come to its attention.

A case in point was Yellow Creek in Middlesboro, Kentucky. There, citizens faced a worsening dilemma during the 1970s. Many of them earned their living at a tannery. For years, the tanning company got rid of chemical waste by dumping it in Yellow Creek. The negative effects of this practice mounted, but leaders did not appear eager to challenge the operation of an employer that meant so much to the local economy. Fish died, as did some of the farm livestock that drank from the stream. Critics compiled evidence of above-average disease rates among creekside residents. At times, the odor eminating from the creek was almost unbearable.

The EPA first got involved in 1980, in a roundabout way. By that year, Middlesboro's city sewage treatment plant was processing waste from the tannery—but not very effectively, according to many citizens. When the time came for the EPA to renew the treatment plant's permit to discharge treated waste, a group called the Yellow Creek Concerned Citizens protested. They claimed the treatment plant was not dealing with the tannery's waste satisfactorily. Further hearings were scheduled, and the Concerned Citizens grew in number.

After a 15-year battle that included a multimillion-dollar lawsuit and EPA enforcement measures, the tannery came under strict regulation and the city built a modern treatment plant. Although the creek bed still is contaminated with poisonous chemical residue, the water has cleared and wildlife has returned.

A Spirit of Responsibility

There is indeed hope. Today, along the Cuyahoga River in Ohio—once branded the river that "oozes rather than flows"—you can see progress toward restoring the river's beauty and usefulness both for wildlife and humans. Pollution has not been banished from the river region, but a partnership of citizen, government, utility, and industry organizations is at work to improve the situation. Research during the 1990s showed reductions in fish deformities caused by chemicals, the gradual return of wildlife such as the Great Blue Heron, and notable other signs of natural recovery. The EPA's involvement has included scientific surveys of the river and surrounding area and funding of rehabilitation projects. In 1998, President Bill Clinton included the Cuyahoga among 14 "American Heritage Rivers," a designation that was expected to spur new environmental and cultural projects.

This is only one example of Americans' efforts, large and small, to take care of our environment. As EPA Administrator Whitman has said, "We have all been entrusted with the stewardship of this shared planet, and it is our responsibility to leave it cleaner for our children and grandchildren."

Glossary

Contaminate—To poison or make unclean.

Ecology—The science of the study of the relationships between all living things and their environment.

Ecosystem—An ecological community and its local, nonbiological community.

Environment—Your surroundings, usually referring to natural surroundings.

Environmentalist—A person concerned about environmental problems and issues.

Epidemic—The widespread outbreak of a contagious disease.

Fertilizer—Natural or synthetic chemicals and compounds applied to crops and flowers to make them grow better and produce more.

Fossil fuels—Coal, oil, and natural gas—compounds formed in the earth during prehistoric times from the remains of plants and animals; they provide most of society's heat and energy today.

Greenhouse effect—A global problem of air pollution created by the trapping of some of the sun's radiation within the earth's atmosphere; one result is that the earth's surface becomes warmer, which can result in climatic changes.

Groundwater—Water stored naturally deep underground, tapped by wells, and providing the source of natural springs.

Habitat—The local environment in which a group of people or wildlife live.

Herbicide—A chemical applied to crops to prevent the growth of weeds and other unwanted plants.

Humus—Decayed, solid animal or plant matter in the soil.

Immune—not susceptible; resistant to a disease-causing agent, or not responsive to the effects of an agent.

Incineration—Burning garbage until it is reduced to ash.

Glossary

Industrial—Relating to or resulting from industry.

Insecticide—A chemical applied to crops to kill insects.

Landfill—A site where solid waste, typically household garbage, is taken to be buried.

Nuclear energy—A method of creating power by splitting the atom, the smallest part of a chemical element.

Organism—A living thing.

Particulates—Chemicals, ash, and other tiny particles that contribute to air pollution.

Pesticide—Pest control chemicals, either herbicides or insecticides.

Photosynthesis—The process by which a green plant uses chemicals in the air and the energy from the sun to create carbohydrates, food and energy for the plant, and releases oxygen into the atmosphere.

Pollution—Contamination of air, water, or soil.

Radiation, radioactivity—The release of potentially harmful waves or particles by nuclear energy production.

Synthetic—Artificially produced, not natural.

Toxin—Poison.

Further Reading

Aylesworth, Thomas G. *Government and the Environment: Tracking the Record*. Hillside, NJ: Enslow Publishers, 1993.

Baines, John. *Environmental Disasters*. New York: Thomson Learning, 1993.

Baird, Nicola. *A Green World?* ("Viewpoints" series). Danbury, CT: Franklin Watts, 1997.

Brown, Joseph E. *Oil Spills: Danger in the Sea*. New York: Dodd, Mead & Company, 1978.

Cherrington, Mark. *Degradation of the Land* ("Earth at Risk" series). New York /Philadelphia: Chelsea House 1992.

Dolan, Edward F. *The American Wilderness and Its Future: Conservation Versus Use*. New York: Franklin Watts, 1992.

Duffy, John. *The Sanitarians: A History of American Public Health*. Urbana, IL: University of Illinois Press, 1990.

Egendorf, Laura K., editor. *Conserving the Environment*. San Diego: Greenhaven Press, 1999.

EPA Web site: *www.epa.gov*

EPA Strategic Plan, September 2000

Haines, Gail Kay. *The Great Nuclear Power Debate*. New York: Dodd, Mead & Company, 1985.

Herda, D.J. *Environmental America: The Northeastern States*. Brookfield, CT: The Millbrook Press, 1991.

Herda, D.J. *Environmental America: The South Central States*. Brookfield, CT: The Millbrook Press, 1991.

Hudson, Kenneth, and Ann Nicholls. *Tragedy on the High Seas: A History of Shipwrecks*. New York: A & W Publishers, 1979.

Kline, Benjamin. *First Along the River: A Brief History of the U.S. Environmental Movement*. San Francisco: Acada Books, 1997.

Marx, Wesley. *The Frail Ocean: A Blueprint for Change in the 1990s and Beyond*. Chester, MA: The Globe Pequot Press, 1991.

Pack, Janet. *Fueling the Future*. Chicago: Childrens Press, 1992.

Pringle, Laurence. *Oil Spills: Damage, Recovery, and Prevention*. New York: Morrow Junior Books, 1993.

Rosenbaum, Walter A. *Energy, Politics, and Public Policy, Second Edition*. Washington, DC: Congressional Quarterly, 1987.

Rothman, Hal K. *Saving the Planet: The American Response to the Environment in the Twentieth Century*. Chicago: Ivan R. Dee, 2000.

Stanley, Phyllis M. *American Environmental Heroes* ["Collective Biographies" series]. Springfield, NJ: Enslow Publishers, 1996.

Stokes, Samuel N., A. Elizabeth Watson, and Shelley S. Mastran. *Saving America's Countryside: A Guide to Rural Conservation, Second Edition*. Baltimore: The Johns Hopkins University Press, 1997.

Index

ABOUT THE AUTHOR: Daniel E. Harmon is an author and editor in Spartanburg, South Carolina. He has written more than thirty nonfiction books, one short story collection, and numerous magazine and newspaper articles. Harmon has served for many years as associate editor of *Sandlapper: The Magazine of South Carolina* and editor of *The Lawyer's PC*, a national computer newsletter published by West Group. His special interests include nautical history and folk music.

SENIOR CONSULTING EDITOR: Arthur M. Schlesinger, jr. is the leading American historian of our time. He won the Pulitzer Prize for his book *The Age of Jackson* (1945) and again for *A Thousand Days* (1965). This chronicle of the Kennedy Administration also won a National Book Award. Professor Schlesinger is the Albert Schweitzer Professor of the Humanities at the City University of New York and has been involved in several other Chelsea House projects, including the REVOLUTIONARY WAR LEADERS and COLONIAL LEADERS series.